First published in America 2019.

ISBN 9780578488172

For more information or to book an event please visit our website at

www.alittleaccounting.com

To my son Johnathan
and my wife Stephanie,
I love you.

Lemonade

Learning accounting
is fun and fast.
It's how we
write down
what happened
in the past.

LEARN ACCOUNTING

A record of business
between you and me,
is what we call
an accounting entry.

A list of entries
from the beginning
to forever,
are written in order
on the general ledger.

GENERAL LEDGER

	To record investment		
		Debit	Credit
Entry #1 Jan 3	Business Expense	$5	
	Cash		$5
	Cups		
Entry #2 Jan 5	Business Expense	$5	
	Cash		$5
	Lemons		

An accounting entry
has two parts,
a debit and a credit
is how it starts.

Debits left first,
then credits down right,
are always the same
in the entries we write.

HOW TO RECORD AN ENTRY

Assets are the things
we love and have,
like buildings, cars, equipment
and always cash.

ASSETS

An asset I get
and will give back eventually,
is credited on the general ledger
as a liability.

Accounting Entry

Debit:	Crayon (Asset)	$1	
Credit:	Crayon (Liability)		$1

LIABILITIES

Owner's Equity says
what is left for me,
after assets subtract
liabilities.

OWNER'S EQUITY

Depreciation is what happens
to assets before long;
use and time
take away value
until the asset is gone.

Accounting Entry

Debit: Depreciation Expense $1
Credit: Accumulated Depreciation $1

DEPRECIATION

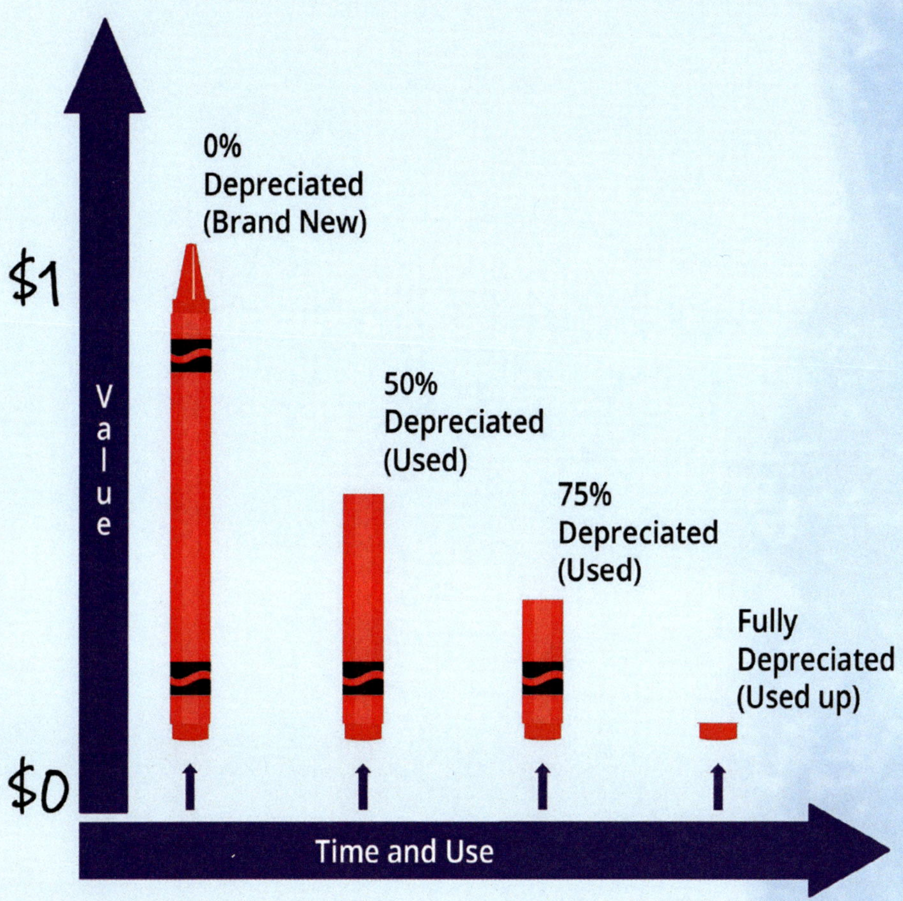

When buying an asset
for me to have,
I debit the asset
and credit my cash.

Accounting Entry

Debit:	Crayon (Asset)	$1	
Credit:	Cash (Asset)		$1

ASSET PURCHASE

When I pay someone back
what they loaned to me,
I credit the asset
and debit the liability.

Accounting Entry

Debit:	Crayon (Liability)	$1	
Credit:	Crayon (Asset)		$1

PAYING OFF LOAN

Credit: Crayon (Asset) $1

Paying for supplies
is quick and fast,
so I debit expense
and credit my cash.

Accounting Entry

Debit:	Lemons (Expense)	$5	
Credit:	Cash (Asset)		$5

EXPENSES

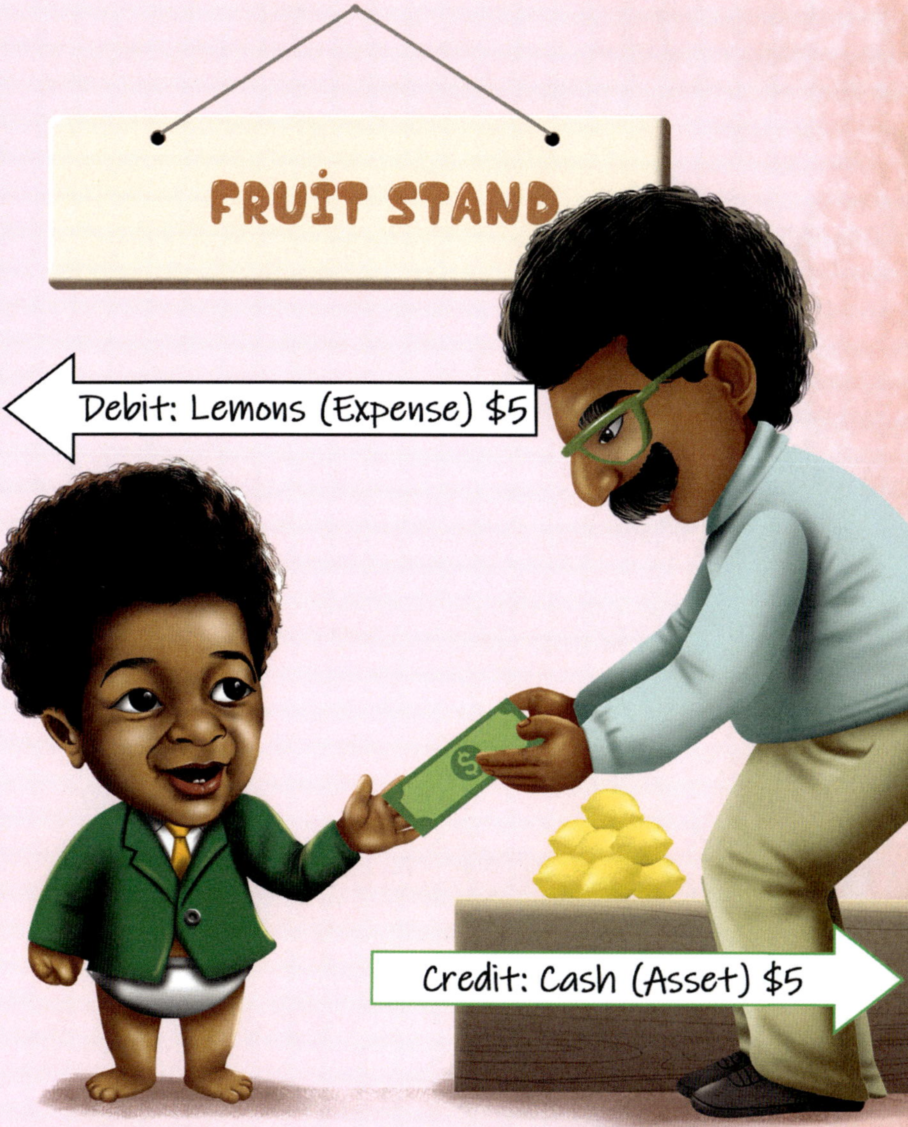
FRUIT STAND
Debit: Lemons (Expense) $5
Credit: Cash (Asset) $5

When I earn some money,
I grab it fast
and always remember
to debit cash.

Now since the money
is meant for me,
I also credit sales revenue
in Owner's Equity.

Accounting Entry

Debit: Cash (Asset) $20
Credit: Sales Revenue (Owner's Equity) $20

EARNING MONEY

All this together
gives a sense,
of how accounting
can be intense.

But little accountants
work hard and smart
to record good business
from the start.

GREAT ACCOUNTING RECORDS

General Ledger

Lemons (Expense) $5
Cash(Asset) $5

Cups(Expense) $5
Cash(Asset) $5

Cash(Asset) $20
Sales Rev(Equity) $20

Food(Expense) $3
Cash(Asset) $3

Crayon(Asset) $1
Crayon loan(Liability) $1

Crayon loan(Liability) $1
Crayon(Asset) $1

GLOSSARY OF TERMS

- **Accounting** - The system of recording business transactions
- **Asset** - Any resource controlled as a result of past efforts that have future economic benefits that are expected to flow to the owner
- **Credit** - An accounting entry made on the right side of an account that increases liability and equity accounts, or decreases asset and expense accounts
- **Debit** - An accounting entry made on the left side of an account that increases asset and expense accounts, or decreases liability and equity accounts
- **Depreciation** - An accounting method of allocating the cost of a physical asset over its useful life that is used to account for declines in value
- **Entry** - A formal record written down that documents a business transaction
- **Expense** - The use of an asset by a business in its operations to produce revenues

- **General Ledger** - The place used to record and store financial transaction details throughout the life of an entity
- **Liability** - A future obligation of an entity where resources are supposed to flow away from the owner to fulfill the obligation requirements
- **Owner's Equity** - The book value of a company, tells how much the owners have rights to after liabilities are subtracted from assets
- **Revenue** - The amount earned by making a sale or providing a service

Assets = Liabilities + Owner's Equity

ABOUT THE AUTHOR

Johnnie Mobley Jr. MBA, PMP

Author J. Mobley (Johnnie Mobley Jr.) is an accountant, consultant and professor. He holds degrees from Pepperdine University and the University of Washington. Johnnie has worked in accounting and finance for more than 10 years with Fortune 500 companies, expanding small businesses and with governmental organizations. Johnnie writes books to help others by promoting financial literacy and business efficiency.

Johnnie uses rhyme and visual examples to explain why understanding financial concepts is important. He also speaks to kids and helps small businesses with their finances and recordkeeping. When he isn't working, Johnnie can be found playing with his family.

Johnnie published his first book, "A Little Accounting" in 2019.

Products and info can be found online at:
www.alittleaccounting.com

Follow us on Twitter @Accounting4kids

Made in the USA
Coppell, TX
09 October 2020